CHINTAN

POEMS FOR LEADERS

DR. SHITAL BADSHAH

Chintan

To my younger brother who has played the role of elder one.

Illustration Credit

Cover design and illustrations for each poem are created by my daughter Rucha Badshah.

She is in her senior year of high school and is an aspiring student of Design.

Advance Praise For Chintan: Poems For Leaders

"Very interesting poems on significant values and qualities to build one's capabilities to be leader through reflection."

- Dr. T. V. Rao, Retd. Professor, *IIM Ahmedabad*

"These poems like a rainbow ,conveying the different shades of leaders true to their vision in every aspect of a person's journey. Poetry can indeed capture the multifaceted nature of leadership, much like a rainbow reveals various colours. Each leader's journey is unique and layered, and poetry has a way of highlighting those nuances beautifully. I found myself deeply engaged by the way they bring to life the essence of leadership through vivid and evocative imagery. The use of poetic language transforms abstract traits into tangible experiences, making the characteristics of leaders feel both personal and universal. The poetic form enriches my understanding by blending art with insight, offering a deeper appreciation of the diverse qualities that define great leaders."

- Dr. Bhawna Gaur, Associate Professor and Head of Case Centre, *Amity University, Dubai*

"Leader is the one who builds the team. He or she takes care of them so they feel comfortable. These poems reflect upon different aspect of leadership and help leaders to touch upon various facets of being leader."

- Chandubhai Virani, Chairman & Managing Director, *Balaji Wafers*

"In addition to the thematic exploration of leadership, these poems stand out for their exceptional quality and poetic craftsmanship. Dr. Shital Badshah's mastery of language and his ability to convey profound insights through the medium of poetry are truly commendable. The poems are not merely a collection of leadership advice, but rather a work of art that invites readers to engage with the subject matter on a deeper, more emotional level. Through the poetic brilliance, he has succeeded in elevating the discourse on leadership, transforming it into a rich, introspective journey that resonates with the heart and the mind. Readers are sure to find themselves captivated and enlightened by the profound wisdom and artistry that permeates the pages of Chintan: Poems for Leaders."

- Dr. Haresh Chaturvedi, Chief Transformation Officer, *GSP Crop Science Pvt Ltd.*

"Congratulations, Dr. Shital Badshah, on your remarkable achievement! Your collection of 52 poems on leadership, complemented by Rucha's illustrations, offers a unique and inspiring perspective. This innovative fusion of poetry and art will undoubtedly resonate with readers seeking both wisdom and beauty in leadership."

- Gaurav VK Singhvi, National Director, *Corporate Connections ® India, Sri Lanka, Nepal*

"I am deeply grateful for the insightful and thought-provoking book by Dr Shital Badshah. This book has been a beacon of guidance, inspiring me to reflect on my leadership journey and strive for excellence. The poignant poems and profound wisdom shared by Dr. Badshah have resonated deeply, encouraging me to cultivate empathy, courage, and vision. Thank you, Dr Shital Badshah, for crafting this masterpiece that will continue to inspire and motivate leaders to make a positive impact."

- Tejas Sheth, Director, *Sheth Brothers*

"Congratulations on your remarkable achievement! Writing a book is a dream come true, and combining leadership poems with your daughter's illustrations makes it even more special. Wishing you great success and good luck with your book's journey!"

- GM Patel, Chairman, *Suryam Group*

"This book is a collection of poems, each with a deep meaning that resonates with various aspects of a leader's journey. Every line and stanza invites you into a space, encouraging self-exploration and introspection. It provides a unique opportunity to learn and grow by examining where you stand and conducting a personal check-in, making it not just a reading experience, but a path to self-discovery and self-improvement."

- Himanshu Patel, Partner, *Samarth Diomand*

"The essence of leadership excellently captured through poems written by Dr. Shital Badshah. A very innovative way of presenting the knowledge on leadership for practitioners."

- Dr. Shubhra Gaur, Registrar, Associate Dean and Professor, *MICA*

"The poems are "shital" and "subtle" to communicate easily about leaders' roles and impact. Poems are empathetic and engaging and a new experience also. With best wishes."

- Unmesh Dixit, Executive Director, *Ahmedabad Management Association*

"My compliments to Dr. Shital Badshah for his outstanding effort in creatively expressing the different facets of leadership through poetry. His suggestion to read and reflect on each facet once a week holds immense potential for fostering inner dialogue and gaining deeper clarity."

- Mayur Patel, Chief Executive Officer, *Proflex (division of M&B Enginering Limited)*

"It is indeed surprising how an educated and qualified scholar in Management and Leadership can write, and that too poetry, without using a single management jargon. The poems resonate with professionals like me and are as grounded as "shital" they are. The sketches convey strong emotions and co-relate with the essence of the poems. The underlying teachings of Bhagwad Geeta ji further enforces their credibility. All in all, easily adaptable by practitioners and those aspiring to be."

- Sunil Jain, President, *Rajoo Engineers Limited*

"Poems for Leaders distills the essence of leadership into 52 thought-provoking poems. A compelling read for those seeking wisdom in verse."

- Hemal Gajjar, Vice President (Human Resources), *Emcure Pharmaceuticals Limited*

"The collection blends simplicity with profound insight, encouraging readers to explore leadership in a personal and reflective way. Each poem offers a unique perspective, challenging traditional management approaches with its artistic touch. It excels in inspiring, introspection and nuanced understanding of leadership. A distinctive and contemplative addition to leadership literature."

- Dr. Shreshtha Dabral, Director, *Academy of Human Resources Development*

"It's simply superb. Each thought and each stanza is quite relatable. As a reader one can feel like yes, this exactly you have gone through. This collection of poems is an indication to everyone that, if you have experienced something unusual, then that is also very normal part of a leadership role, which you are playing. This book is nothing but the experiential journey which the author has traveled so far in the domain of leadership. Kudos to Rucha for precise visual articulation of words."

- Viral Vaishnav, Chief Administrative Officer and Incharge Registrar, *PlastIndia International University*

Foreword

Does a book of poems need a forward!

Well, it is not just a book of poems in the traditional sense we know of poetry. The poet generally has an outpour of his or her emotions and that becomes his or her poems.

Here, each poem has a purpose. It is written with an objective in view.

This is a collection of poems for leaders. Generally, business leaders get little time to reflect on their own emotions.

Each poem is small, only a few words.

'Brevity is soul of wits.' This is more than true when we read this collection.

The poet, through his experiences and reflection, made an effort, for you the reader, to experience and reflect. It is an emotionally serious job.

I wish and pray this maiden venture of words with pictures meets with success!

With each poem, there is a picture which depicts the reality in a more concrete shape and form.

This will give the reader better opportunity to feel, to think and to understand his own reality. May God bless you both!

Dr. DM Pestonjee
Retd. Professor (Indian Insitute of Management - Ahmedabad)

Preface

The subject of leadership is as old as mankind. It is as simple as one feels, and as complex as one makes.

I got a chance to study many articles, research papers, and books during my doctoral research (PhD program).

What I learnt,

Leadership is an art than a science.
Then, why not to present in art form.
Here it is.
52 poems representing different facets of leadership.

I prefer the reader to make their own meaning of each poem.

Read one poem at a time, every week. Each word, each stanza. Give your own meaning to it, write it next to the poem for your future reference.

It may also happen that every time you read the same poem, you will have different meaning to it. Because, all poems are reflections of life.

Life is contextual. Give meaning to it.

Not a single management jargon is mentioned in any
poem, but you will find all of them in all poems.
Happy leading.

Dr. Shital Badshah

Leadership is complex,
Until *you* make it simple.

You may not agree with what I say
You may not see what I foresee

But, have trust
Because I trust you

Miracles do happen
Change do take place

With me
With
you
With us

For better tomorrow.

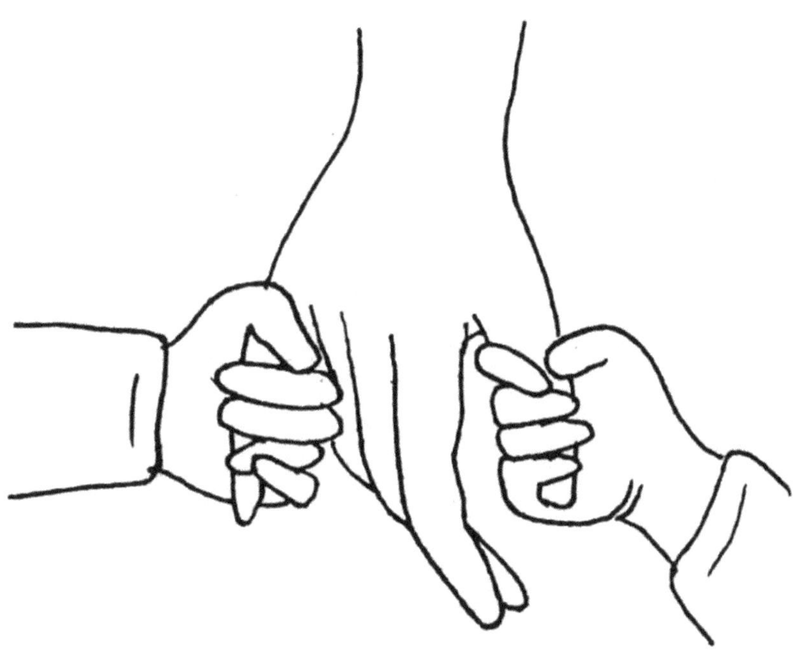

I am like pure gold
I am like clean water

I don't have any shade of grey
I flow with the flow

No modification
No manipulation

I am here just for the well-being of the higher being.

Believe in when the time is not favorable
Believe in when the circumstance is not aligned
Believe in when the odds are against you

Believe in because you are human being
Believe in because you can fail
Believe in because you can succeed.

No one has wings
No one can fly

But plane makes you fly
From one place to another
From here to there

It took long since
The first plane was made
To your first flight

Give it time
Give it space

One day
You will have wings
You will fly.

Sometimes I feel I own my thoughts
The other times I feel they own me

Sitting in my office I reach to another place
Another city, another desk

The river, ocean, mountain and jungle
The country looks smaller, even the continent

Maybe my office has an impact on me
The chair has something

Sometimes I feel I own my thoughts.

Faith

It is not easy to have
My mind is rational

I check
For validity

I check
For authenticity

I check
For proof

I check
For logic

But people
Don't come with rationality
all the time

I must have faith
In them
In me.

When emotions are high
Words play the game

Do not allow your words
To tumble and injure

They may not come back again
Like an arrow and the train

Ensure the heart is at the front
Mind an inch behind

It will take you miles ahead

When emotions are high
Do not play the game.

Praise for tomorrow
Not for today

From the heart, not from the mind
Not for the sake of doing it

Admire for the efforts
Results are eventual

People may forget the occasion
And, rewards are also temporary

The gesture of appraising
Openly
Genuinely
In front of others
In front of the
team
Should come from the heart
And not from the mind.

Needs change

From time to time
From age to age
From stage to stage

What was important yesterday
May not be relevant today
May look insignificant tomorrow

Learn about the aspiration
For the person
For the team

Show them the path
For better destination

Help them define
The right destination

It is not about the needs
The needs change

From time to time
From age to age
From stage to stage.

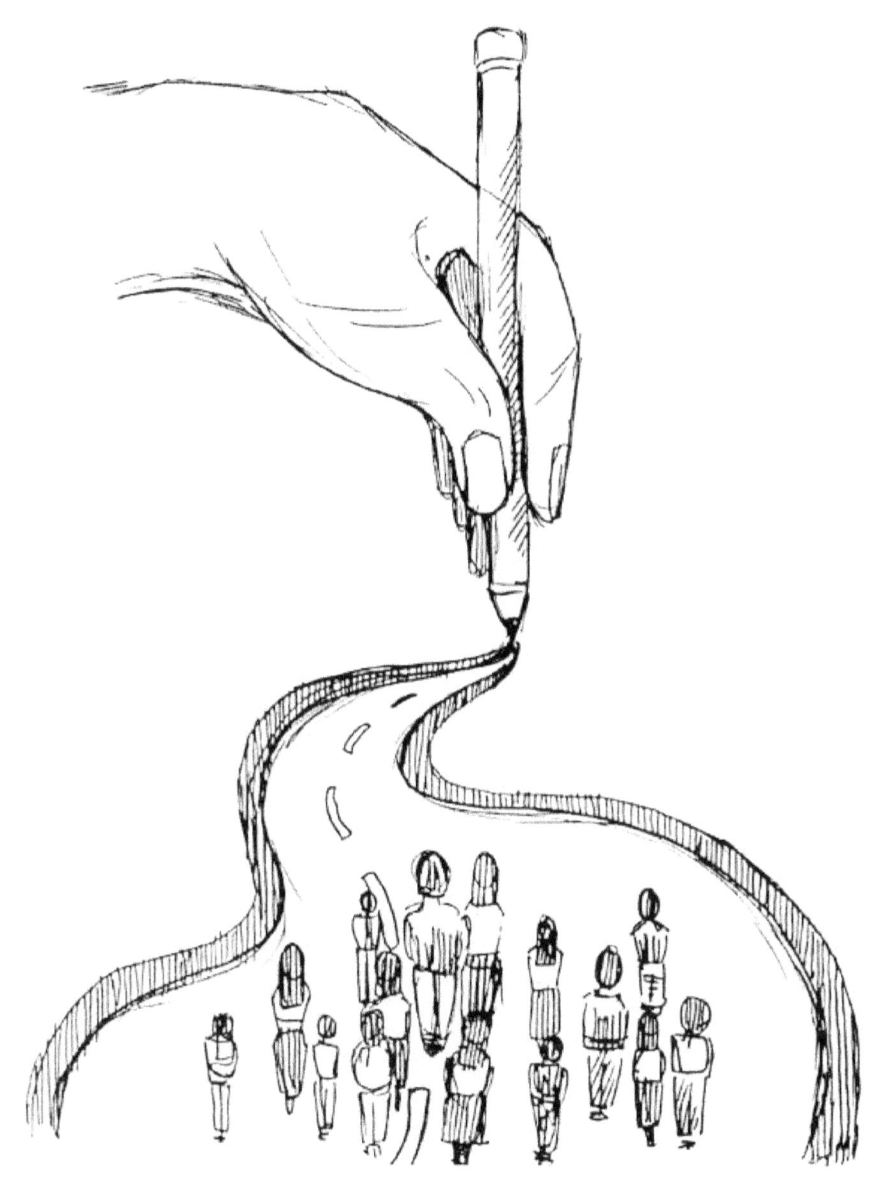

If you are not certain
Do not promise

Once done
Follow it

Your words are important
They create universe around you

May not be visible to
you But others can see it
They can feel it

That universe is bigger than you
For them

Interestingly,
It is not visible to you.

You are being observed
You are being followed
You are being emulated
You are being imitated

What you do
What you speak

How you behave
How you act

You say, they magnify
You listen, they glorify

Your values
Your ethics
Your thoughts

You are role model to them.

The thread in necklace
The electricity in wire
The soul in body

Not visible apparently
But their existence matters
Individually
They are different
Competent and skilled
Your presence
Gives them collective strength
And will

Direction to progress
Sense of belongingness
Inter-dependence with
Independence

Identity, collective
Freedom to experiment.

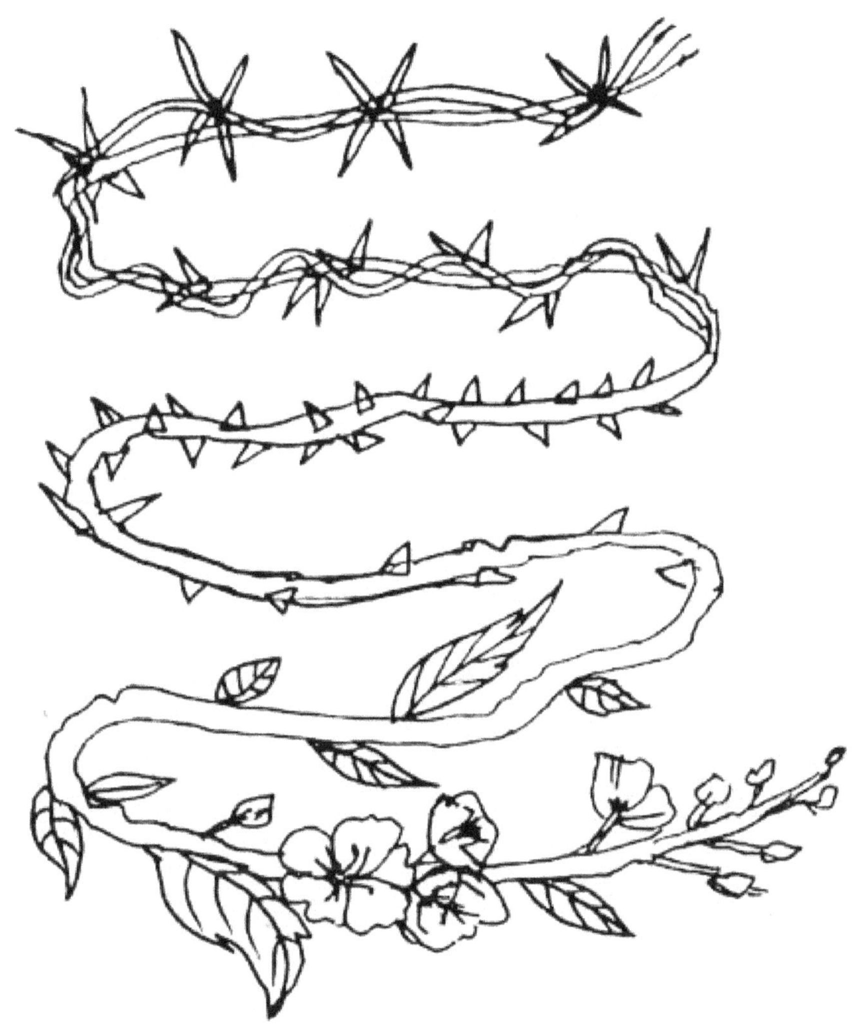

Enjoy the current moment
Tomorrow is illusion
Yesterday is delusion

Joy, happiness, sorrow and sadness
Part of life, part of game

Things may not be governed
Nor does the life

Be with the stream
Sometimes against it

Let the mettle get tested
With a smile on the face

Enjoy the current momen

NoW
Now
NoW
Now
NoW
Now
NoW
Now
Now
NoW
NoW
Now

What is this for?

Let it have meaning in life
Let the life have meaning to live
Do not be one among all
Let it be small but impactful
Let the world notice you
Even if it is small

The value you add
The lives you change
Has some relevance
Not to many, maybe to few

Ever lasting and
Permanent

Not superfluous,
Not momentary.

Switch off
It is required

Turning your mind to something else
Onto more important priorities
Onto more important aspects of life

Preserving energy for better tomorrow
Not letting it get drained

Having macro perspective of the canvas
Without getting confused with micro
perspective

Creating balance between past, present and tomorrow.

Complexity, ambiguity, entropy,
randomness I wonder
Is it the situation or
My nature?

Deep down somewhere
I am alone

Not because I don't like people
Not because I am not friendly
Not because I am not social

But because
I have preserved my identity
I have made that choice
Of not being
What I am not

I like aloneness
With
My originality.

I like to make mistakes by trusting others
I like to fail by trusting others
I like to be fooled by trusting others

Because it is not about them
It is more about me

I will trust
Unconditionally.

I will prefer to be known as
Hard core negotiator
Than someone with weak heart

I will prefer to grab my own pie
Worthy of everything
Than be known as poor guy

I will prefer to look straight into
Eyes of next person
Than make stories about

I will go the extra mile for everything
Which makes me comfortable in

Playing my role perfectly.

Being subjective
Is human

Objectivity can be handy

I deal more with human
Than robots

It is okay to be subjective
Than objective

In fact,
I am human too.

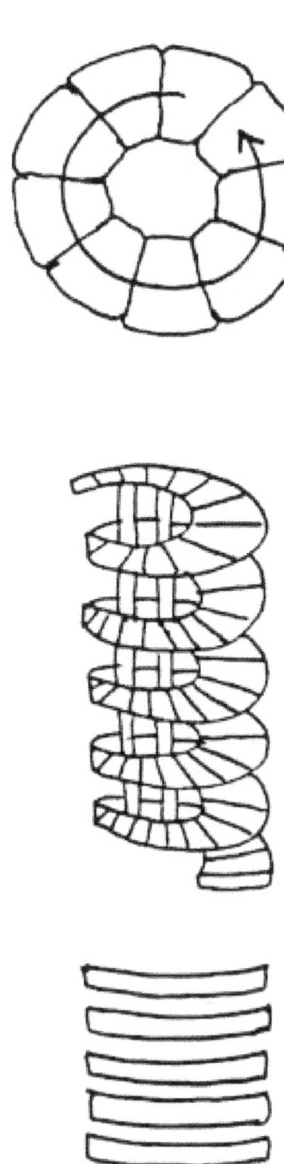

What did you say,
I can not do?

Oh my friend,
It is more about you
Than me
I appreciate your opinion
I value and respect
I listen and ponder

But, after all,
It is just an opinion
It does not define me
I feel
I can do

And,
I will.

I want to rise, but not alone
I want to grow, but not alone
I want to fly, but not alone

With you, I feel
More comfortable

With you, I feel
More passionate

With you, I feel
More dedicated

I want to contribute
In your life
Today and tomorrow

Let us make it our journey
Not mine or yours.

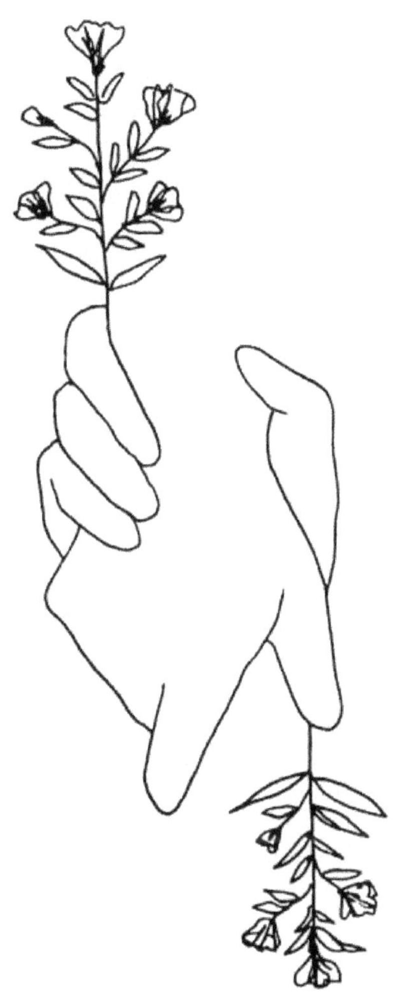

Who makes the decision?

I will be happy
If you make the decision

I empower you
For the efforts
For the decision

If you succeed
It is yours

If you fail
I own the responsibility

Just remember one thing,
Keep moving.

Negativity, helplessness, frustration, pessimism
Disapproval, rejection, unpredictability, volatility
Fickleness, irregularity, instability, impulsiveness
Suddenness, recklessness, irresponsibility,
insensitivity

That is not me.

Let us fight
For the purpose
Not with the person

The person may change
So does the situation

Let the purpose be supreme
Here and there

No baggage, no carrying it forward
New day will arrive
New results will be achieved

Let the purpose and the person
Be with you.

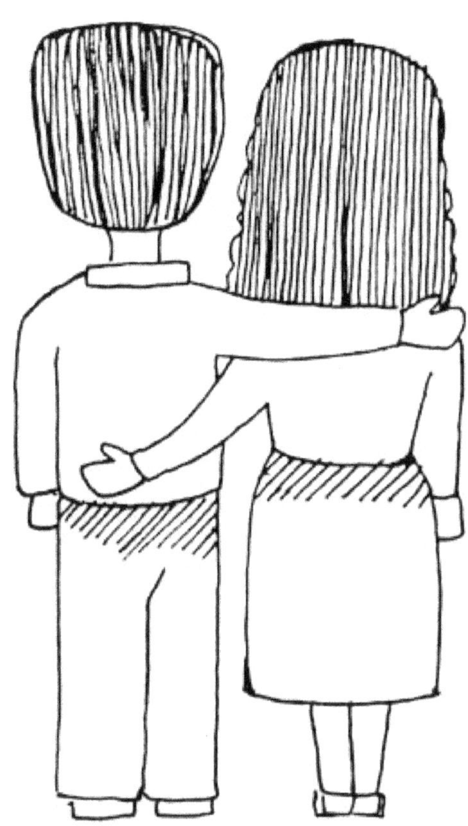

Limitations
In psychological plane or real one

They are there to revise you
A better one, A newer one

Change is universal
Water, earth, fire, air
Keep moving, keep changing

It is not the destination you enjoy
It is the journey you cherish

Higher you go
Wider you see
The canvas becomes larger
So does your vision

Overcome your limitations
To widen your horizon.

Neither you nor me
Our relationship matters

What you carry on the table
What I carry on the table
Is indicatory

What we carry in our heart
Makes what we contribute
In our relationship

The transaction may be
Temporary
It will fade away with
Time
After a time
What we remember
Is behavior

Yours and mine
Mine and yours.

Failed?
Bounce back.

The situation may be adverse
The odds may be against you

There is someone out there waiting for you
To tumble
To crash
To finish

But believe me

Someone within you is waiting for you
To rise again
To regain what you have lost
To establish your legacy

Forever.

Never judge
Anyone

What you see is only
One dimension

You have your own lens
Which may have spots

Go closer
Go deeper

And,
You may find the curtain
Which your lens could not remove

And, here is
A whole new world
For you.

Compete fiercely
That defines you

Go aggressive
While you form your strategy

Ensure for excellence
While you execute

Be rowdy
While you deal with the numbers
At the same time
Take care of people
While you deal with them.

Write your own script
Original and unique

Not copied nor borrowed
Not stolen from anywhere

Some parts simple
Some complex
Some confusing
Some puzzling
But
Neither modified
Nor amended

Original and unique

You are the writer
You are the player

Of the game
That is life.

LIFE

Time

Sometimes, it may not be on your side
The other times, it takes your side

Few times, it flies at speed of light
The other times, it slows down with no light

At times, with no reason, it gives you results
At other times, you don't have any reason for not getting results

Is it a friend
Or Foe

Maybe both, at times

May you wish to dictate it
May you wish to dominate it
May you wish to govern it

But don't forget
It is time, never conquered by anyone, anytime.

I don't know where to go
Am I lost or the journey is so

More clarity I wish
More confusion I
receive

The spiral of confusion
Is part of my life
The up I go
The down I feel

The cost of being at the top
Is sometimes too high.

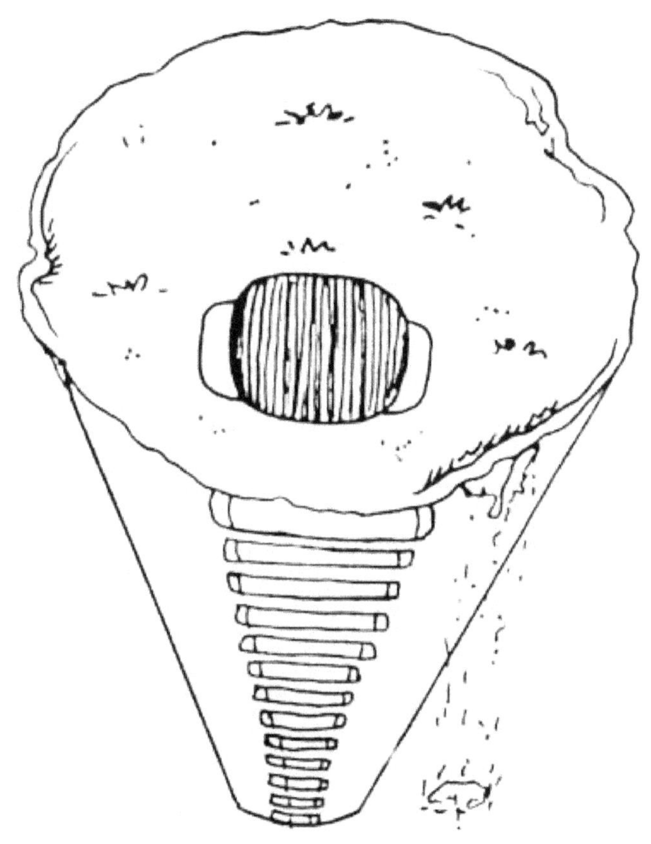

In the middle of the sea
And at the shore

I am the one
Who wishes to
go

To explore new things
To test my skills
To upgrade myself
To lift my soul

If you are like me
Pack your bags

Open your mind
For togetherness

Let us experiment
Let us check

Whether the sea is deep or
Our frequencies match.

Perfection
Precision
Flawlessness

I believe in them
Not because I am obsessed with them
But, I believe the game starts with them
To let the world know
I am different
I am unique

I am here to give you
Perfection
Precision
Flawlessness.

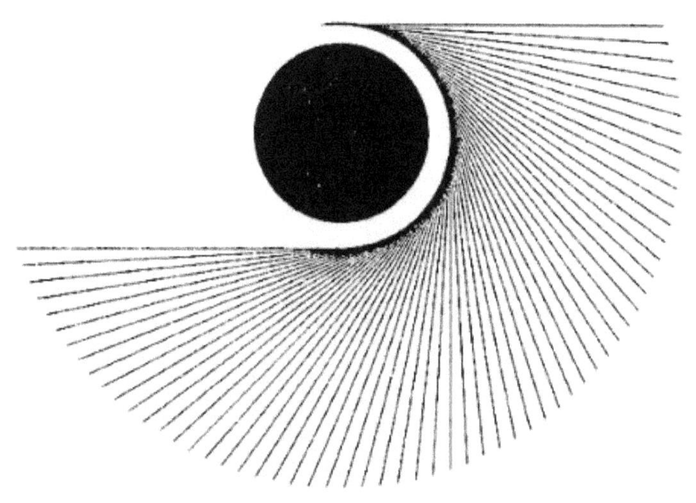

Purity is inherent
Additives are external.

Inquire
When you are confused

The status quo is like
A small boat in the ocean

It is as safe as
the size of the wave

The existence of paddle
Is in fact, immaterial

As is the acceptance of
The status quo

Rise against the tide
What matters is the will
Not the paddle.

The words are not important
The context is

We are different
Use different words
Assumption is an enemy
Silence is a friend

Do not let emotions
Ride for free

You pay the price
And bear the cost

Instead, select the words
Which set the context right.

Universal truth
Unshakable belief
Unconditional promise

It becomes once I commit

The situation maybe adverse
Not my determination

Sometimes it takes longer
Than anticipated
To deliver
To make one happy

But at the end
My character gives me strength
To do more in life.

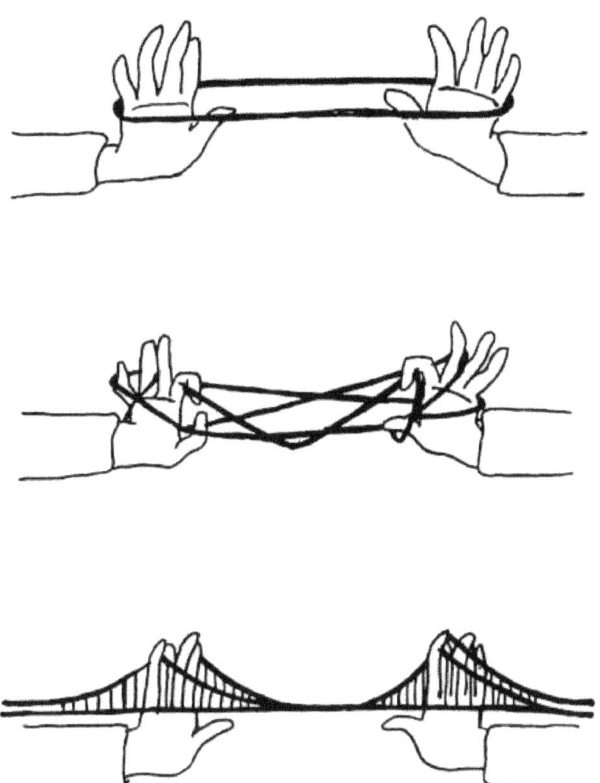

My shadow on the floor today
May not talk about
My perspiration

But my shoes do talk about
My journey
The hardships of
My journey

The thin and lean I have gone
The baggage I have lost

One needs to compare
My shadow on the floor today
With the one when I started.

Frustration
Requires
Coping mechanism.

Not knowing
The right coping mechanism
Eventually
Leads to
More frustration.

While I walk down the lane
My childhood comes to my mind

My aspirations, my dreams
My love in sight

Same houses, same windows
Same birds, and same poles
Goes here and stand there
Everything is same
Except me

There I see that old banyan tree
Today, it looks younger than me.

The silence of the room
The darkness of the mind

The lack of intent
The absence of new line

For someone a killing moment
For someone a rising one

The map is same
The travellers are different.

Is it about the height

The more I go up
The less people I find there

Or I don't know
The art of getting there

The journey is painful
Not everyone can manage it

Maybe it is the cost
Of getting there

I wish someone would have
Shown me the cost prior.

That small bird
Weaving its nest

A few thin threads
One at a time

No formal education
No formal training

The nest is small
The purpose is big

It is not for many years
But, certainly
Two generations do surviv

Focusing on one aspect of the matter
Leaving others on its own

Thinking that it would take care of it on its own
Instead, I have damaged it on my own

I was waiting someone to own
But I forgot that someone couldn't own

How could I leave others on its own
When everyone just looked at me to own.

I feel free when I give
The freedom to think and act on one's own

I feel free when I empower
Others to make their existence more meaningful

I feel free when I delegate
Important tasks so they feel important

I feel free when I leave
The ownership which I anyhow don't own.

Keep climbing
Even if no one is around

Keep climbing
Even if the summit is not visible

Keep climbing
Even if the road is not clear

Keep climbing
Because you have a zeal to challenge yourself

Keep climbing
Because you know you can do it

Keep climbing
Because you wish to meet yourself over there.

There is everyone in me

Kansh, Ravan, Duryodhan, and Shakuni
Arjun, Ram, Hanuman, and Krishna

I will let you decide whom you want to
meet It is your choice.

Sometimes I ignore
Purposefully

I do not have solution for
Everything

I am human
And I know it

Let time
Play its supreme role
Purposefully.

12
1
11
2
10
3
9
4
8
5
7
6

I feel good
When I am being heard

I feel good
When I am being involved

I feel good
When I am being acknowledged

I reciprocate the same
Unconditionally.

This may be the last
At this point in time

But the timeline is
Long and continuous

I will remain in the game
For the game

I am just part of it,
And not the game.

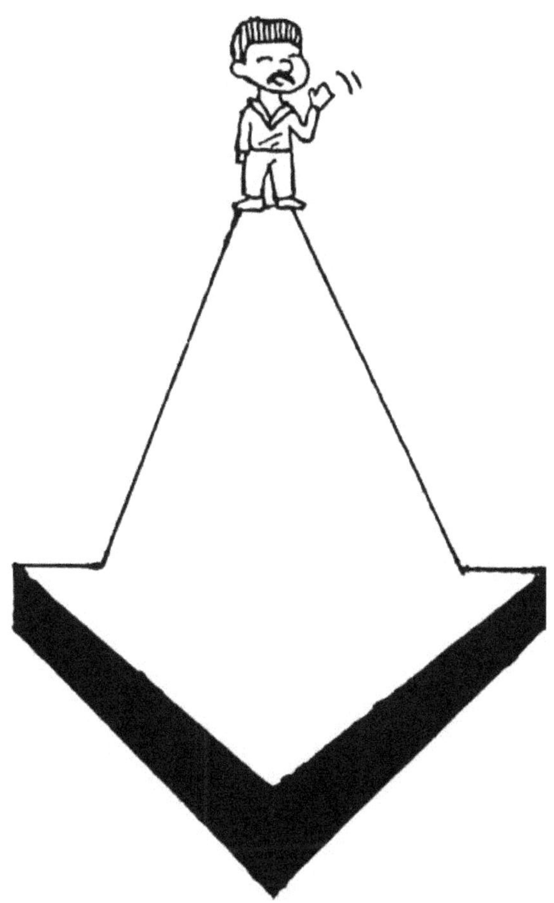

About The Author

Dr. Shital Badshah

An engineer by chance, management graduate by experiment, and PhD holder by choice.

Dr. Shital Badshah is a Leadership Coach, who helps senior management executives to become better leaders, so they can lead themselves, their teams, and their organisations successfully.

He has contributed in the development of many senior people at multinational companies, family businesses, and entrepreneur driven companies. He has vast experience in Leadership Development, Change Management, Culture Development, Strategic Leadership, Team Development and Organisation Development.

Dr. Badshah completed his PhD in the field of Leadership under the guidance of Dr. DM Pestonjee, who was a professor at Indian Institute of Management, Ahmedabad, and underwent certification program on Executive Coaching from Indian Institute of Management, Bangalore.

He works as Independent Director at leading listed companies of Gujarat.

He is the founder of Growth Catalyst (www.GrowthCatalystIndia.com), that designs unique experiential learning solutions for senior leaders.

Dr. Badshah is a student of Indian classical music, and a cyclist by passion. He has a keen interest in Vedic Astrology since his childhood, and is practicing it across many countries.